GW00374630

Pope B

Be disciples
of Christ

Homilies and Addresses in Brazil

All booklets are published thanks to the
generous support of the members of the
Catholic Truth Society

CATHOLIC TRUTH SOCIETY
PUBLISHERS TO THE HOLY SEE

2

Contents

'The Pope therefore wants to say to all of you: The Church is our home! This is our home! In the Catholic Church we find all that is good, all that gives grounds for security and consolation! Anyone who accepts Christ, "the way, the truth and the life" in his totality is assured of peace and happiness, in this life and in the next!' (12 May 2007).

Do you want Life?

"If you would be perfect, go, sell what you possess and give to the poor…and come, follow me" (*Mt* 19:21).

1. I was particularly eager to include a meeting with you young people during my first journey to Latin America… I have always felt a very special joy at these encounters. I remember especially the *Twentieth World Youth Day* at which I was able to preside two years ago in Germany. Some of you gathered here today were also present! It is an emotional memory for me on account of the abundant fruits of the Lord's grace poured out upon those who were there. Among the many fruits which I could point to, there is little doubt that the first was the exemplary sense of fraternity that stood as a clear witness to the Church's perennial vitality throughout the world.

2. For this reason, my dear friends, I am certain that today the same impressions I received in Germany will be renewed here. In 1991, during his visit to Mato Grosso, the Servant of God Pope John Paul II, of venerable memory, said that "youth are the first protagonists of the third millennium … they are the

ones who will be charged with the destiny of this
new phase in human history" (16 October 1991).
Today, I feel moved to make the same observation
regarding all of you.

The Christian life you lead in numerous
parishes and small ecclesial communities, in
universities, colleges and schools, and most of all,
in places of work both in the city and in the
countryside, is undoubtedly pleasing to the Lord.
But it is necessary to go even further. We can
never say "enough", because the love of God is
infinite, and the Lord asks us – or better – requires
us to open our hearts wider so that there will be
room for even more love, goodness, and
understanding for our brothers and sisters, and for
the problems which concern not only the human
community, but also the effective preservation and
protection of the natural environment of which we
are all a part. "Our forests have more life": do not
allow this flame of hope which your National
Hymn places on your lips to die out. The
devastation of the environment in the Amazon
Basin and the threats against the human dignity of
peoples living within that region call for greater
commitment in the different areas of activity than
society tends to recognize.

What must I do?

3. Today I would like to reflect on the text we have just heard from Saint Matthew (cf. 19:16-22). It speaks of a young man who ran to see Jesus. His impatience merits special attention. In this young man I see all of you young people of Brazil and Latin America. You have "run" here from various regions of this Continent for this meeting of ours. You want to listen to the words of Jesus himself – spoken through the voice of the Pope.

You have a crucial question – a question that appears in this Gospel – to put to him. It is the same question posed by the young man who ran to see Jesus: *What good deed must I do, to have eternal life?* I would like to take a deeper look at this question with you. It has to do with life. A life which – in all of you – is exuberant and beautiful. What are you to do with it? How can you live it to the full?

We see at once that in the very formulation of the question, the "here" and "now" are not enough; to put it another way, we cannot limit our life within the confines of space and time, however much we might try to broaden their horizons. Life transcends them. In other words: we want to live, not die. We have a sense of something telling us that life is eternal and that we must apply ourselves to reach it.

In short, it rests in our hands and is dependent, in a certain way, on our own decision.

The question in the Gospel does not regard only the future. It does not regard only a question about what will happen after death. On the contrary, it exists as a task in the present, in the "here" and "now", which must guarantee authenticity and consequently the future. In short, the young man's question raises the issue of life's meaning. It can therefore be formulated in this way: what must I do so that my life has meaning? How must I live so as to reap the full fruits of life? Or again: what must I do so that my life is not wasted?

Jesus alone can give us the answer, because he alone can guarantee us eternal life. He alone, therefore, can show us the meaning of this present life and give it fullness.

Why do you ask?

4. But before giving his response, Jesus asks about a very important aspect of the young man's enquiry: why do you ask me about what is good? In this question, we find the key to the answer. This young man perceives that Jesus is good and that he is a teacher – a teacher who does not deceive. We are here because we have the very same conviction: Jesus is good. It may be that we do not know how to

explain fully the reason for this perception, but it undoubtedly draws us to him and opens us up to his teaching: he is a good teacher. To recognize the good means to love. And whoever loves – to use a felicitous expression of Saint John – knows God (cf. 1 *Jn* 4:7). The young man in the Gospel has perceived God in Jesus Christ.

Jesus assures us that God alone is good. To be open to goodness means to receive God. In this way, he invites us to see God in all things and in everything that happens, even where most people see only God's absence. When we see the beauty of creation and recognize the goodness present there, it is impossible not to believe in God and to experience his saving and reassuring presence. If we came to see all the good that exists in the world – and moreover, experience the good that comes from God himself – we would never cease to approach him, praise him, and thank him. He continually fills us with joy and good things. His joy is our strength.

Do you want life?

But we can only know in an imperfect, partial way. To understand what is good, we need help, which the Church offers us on many occasions, especially through catechesis. Jesus himself shows what is good for us by giving us the first element in his catechesis:

"If you would enter life, keep the commandments" (*Mt* 19:17). He begins with the knowledge that the young man has surely already acquired from his family and from the synagogue: he knows the commandments. These lead to life, which means that they guarantee our authenticity. They are the great signs which lead us along the right path. Whoever keeps the commandments is on the way that leads to God.

It is not enough, however, simply to know them. Witness is even more important than knowledge; or rather, it is applied knowledge. The commandments are not imposed upon us from without; they do not diminish our freedom. On the contrary: they are strong internal incentives leading us to act in a certain way. At the heart of them we find both grace and nature, which do not allow us to stay still. We must walk. We are motivated to do something in order fulfil our potential. To find fulfilment through action is, in reality, to become real. To a large extent, from the time of our youth, we are whatever we want to be. We are, so to speak, the work of our own hands.

The fears you have

5. At this point, I turn once more to you, young people, because I want to hear you give the same response that the young man in the Gospel gave: all these I have observed from my youth. The young

man in the Gospel was good. He kept the commandments. He was walking along the way of God. Jesus, therefore, gazing at him, loved him. By recognizing that Jesus was good, he showed that he too was good. He had an experience of goodness, and therefore of God. And you, young people of Brazil and Latin America, have you already discovered what is good? Do you follow the Lord's commandments? Have you discovered that this is the one true road to happiness?

These years of your life are the years which will prepare you for your future. Your "tomorrow" depends much on how you are living the "today" of your youth. Stretching out in front of you, my dear young friends, is a life that all of us hope will be long; yet it is only one life, it is unique: do not let it pass it vain; do not squander it. Live it with enthusiasm and with joy, but most of all, with a sense of responsibility.

Many times, we who are pastors feel a sense of trepidation as we take stock of the situation in today's world. We hear talk of the fears of today's youth. These fears reveal an enormous lack of hope: a fear of death, at the very moment when life is blossoming and the young are searching to find how to fulfil their potential; fear of failure, through not having discovered the meaning of life; fear of remaining detached in the face of a disconcerting acceleration of events and communications. We see the high death rate among young people, the threat of violence, the deplorable proliferation of drugs which strike at the deepest roots of youth today. For these reasons, we hear talk of a "lost youth".

Be apostles of youth

But as I gaze at you young people here present – you who radiate so much joy and enthusiasm – I see you as Christ sees you: with a gaze of love and trust, in the certainty that you have found the true way. You are the youth of the Church. I send you out, therefore, on the great mission of evangelizing young men and women who have gone astray in this world like sheep without a shepherd. *Be apostles of youth.* Invite them to walk with you, to have the same experience of faith, hope, and love; to encounter Jesus so that they may feel truly loved, accepted, able to realize their full potential. May they too discover the sure ways of the commandments, and, by following them, come to God.

You can be the builders of a new society if you seek to put into practice a conduct inspired by universal moral values, but also a personal commitment to a vitally important human and spiritual formation. Men and women who are ill-prepared for the real challenges presented by a correct interpretation of the Christian life in their own surroundings will easily fall prey to all the assaults of materialism and secularism, which are more and more active at all levels.

Be free and responsible

Be men and women who are free and responsible; make the family a centre that radiates peace and joy; be promoters of life, from its beginning to its natural end; protect the elderly, since they deserve respect and admiration for the good they have done. The Pope also expects young people to seek to sanctify their work, carrying it out with technical skill and diligence, so as to contribute to the progress of all their brothers and sisters, and to shed the light of the Word upon all human activities (cf. *Lumen Gentium*, 36). But above all, the Pope wants them to set about building a more just and fraternal society, fulfilling their duties towards the State: respecting its laws; not allowing themselves to be swept along by hatred and violence; seeking to be an example of Christian conduct in their professional and social milieu, distinguishing themselves by the integrity of their social and professional relationships. They should remember that excessive ambition for wealth and power leads to corruption of oneself and others; there are no valid motives that would justify attempting to impose one's own worldly aspirations – economic or political – through fraud and deceit.

There exists, in the final analysis, an immense panorama of action in which questions of a social, economic and political nature take on particular importance, as long as they draw their inspiration from the Gospel and the social teaching of the Church. This includes building a more just and fraternal society, reconciled and at peace, it includes the commitment to reduce violence, initiatives to promote the fullness of life, the democratic order and the common good and especially initiatives aimed at eliminating certain forms of discrimination existing in Latin American societies: avoiding exclusion, for the sake of mutual enrichment.

Respect and honour marriage

Above all, have great respect for the institution of the sacrament of Matrimony. There cannot be true domestic happiness unless, at the same time, there is fidelity between spouses. Marriage is an institution of natural law, which has been raised by Christ to the dignity of a sacrament; it is a great gift that God has given to mankind: respect it and honour it. At the same time, God calls you to respect one another when

you fall in love and become engaged, since conjugal
life, reserved by divine ordinance to married couples,
will bring happiness and peace only to the extent that
you are able to build your future hopes upon chastity,
both within and outside marriage. I repeat here to all
of you that "*eros* tends to rise . . . towards the Divine,
to lead us beyond ourselves; yet for this very reason it
calls for a path of ascent, renunciation, purification
and healing" (Encyclical Letter *Deus Caritas Est*, 5). To
put it briefly, it requires a spirit of sacrifice and
renunciation for the sake of a greater good, namely
the love of God above all things. Seek to resist
forcefully the snares of evil that are found in many
contexts, driving you towards a dissolute and
paradoxically empty life, causing you to lose the
precious gift of your freedom and your true
happiness. True love "increasingly seeks the happiness
of the other, is concerned more and more with the
beloved, bestows itself and wants to 'be there for' the
other" (*ibid.*, 7) and therefore will always grow in
faithfulness, indissolubility and fruitfulness.

Think of your vocation

In all these things, count upon the help of Jesus
Christ who will make them possible through his grace
(cf. *Mt* 19:26). The life of faith and prayer will lead
you along the paths of intimacy with God, helping

you to understand the greatness of his plans for every person. "For the sake of the kingdom of heaven" (*Mt* 19:12), some are called to a total and definitive self-giving, by consecrating themselves to God in the religious life – an "exceptional gift of grace", as the Second Vatican Council expressed it (cf. Decree *Perfectae Caritatis*, 12). Consecrated persons, by giving themselves totally to God, prompted by the Holy Spirit, participate in the Church's mission, bearing witness before all people to their hope in the heavenly Kingdom. I therefore bless and invoke divine protection upon all those religious who have dedicated themselves to Christ and to their brothers and sisters within the vineyard of the Lord. Consecrated persons truly deserve the gratitude of the ecclesial community: monks and nuns, contemplative men and women, religious men and women dedicated to apostolic works, members of Secular Institutes and Societies of Apostolic Life, hermits and consecrated virgins. "Their existence witnesses to their love for Christ as they walk the path proposed in the Gospel and with deep joy commit themselves to the same style of life which he chose for himself" (Congregation for Institutes of Consecrated Life and for Societies of Apostolic Life, Instruction *Starting Afresh from Christ*, 5). I pray that in this moment of grace and profound communion in Christ, the Holy

Spirit will awaken in the hearts of many young people an impassioned love, prompting them to follow and imitate Jesus Christ, chaste, poor and obedient, totally devoted to the glory of the Father and to love for their brothers and sisters.

What to make of your life?

6. The Gospel assures us that the young man who went to meet Jesus was very rich. We may understand this wealth not only on the material level. Youth itself is a singular treasure. We have to discover it and to value it. Jesus appreciated it so much that he went on to invite the young man to participate in his saving mission. He had great potential and could have accomplished great things.

But the Gospel goes on to say that this young man, having heard the invitation, was saddened. He went away downcast and sad. This episode causes us to reflect further on the treasure of youth. It is not, in the first place, a question of material wealth, but of life itself, and the values inherent in youth. This wealth is inherited from two sources: life, transmitted from generation to generation, at the ultimate origin of which we find God, full of wisdom and love; and upbringing, which locates us within a culture, to such an extent that we might almost say we are more children of culture and therefore of faith, than of nature. From life springs freedom, which manifests itself, especially in this phase, as responsibility. There comes the great moment of decision, in a twofold choice: firstly, concerning one's state of life, and secondly concerning one's profession. It is about providing an answer to the question: what do I do with my life?

Do not be cowards

In other words, youth appears as a form of wealth because it leads to the discovery of life as a gift and a task. The young man in the Gospel understood that his youth was itself a treasure. He went to Jesus, the good Teacher, in order to seek some direction. At the moment of the great decision, however, he lacked the courage to wager everything on Jesus Christ. In consequence, he went away sad and downcast. This is what happens whenever our decisions waver and become cowardly and self-seeking. He understood that what he lacked was generosity, and this did not allow him to realize his full potential. He withdrew to his riches, turning them to selfishness.

Jesus regretted the sadness and the cowardice of the young man who had come to seek him out. The Apostles, like all of you here today, filled the vacuum left by that young man who went away sad and downcast. They, and we, are happy, because we know the one in whom we believe (cf. *2 Tim* 1:12). We know and we bear witness with our lives that he alone has the words of eternal life (cf. *Jn* 6:68). Therefore, we can exclaim with Saint Paul: Rejoice always in the Lord! (cf. *Phil* 4:4).

Do not waste your youth

7. My appeal to you today, young people present at this gathering, is this: *do not waste your youth*. Do not seek to escape from it. Live it intensely. Consecrate it to the high ideals of faith and human solidarity.

You, young people, are not just the future of the Church and of humanity, as if we could somehow run away from the present. On the contrary: you are that young man now; you are that young man in the Church and in humanity today. You are his young face. The Church needs you, as young people, to manifest to the world the face of Jesus Christ, visible in the Christian community. Without this young face, the Church would appear disfigured. ...

Be saints for today

My dear young friends, like the young man in the Gospel who asked Jesus: *"What good deed must I do, to have eternal life?"*, you are all seeking ways to respond generously to God's call. I pray that you may listen to his saving words and that you may become his witnesses for the peoples of today. May God pour out upon all of you his blessings of peace and joy.

My dear young people, Christ is calling you to be saints. He himself is inviting you and wants to walk with you, in order to enliven with his Spirit the steps that Brazil is taking at the beginning of this third millennium of the Christian era. I ask the *Senhora Aparecida* to guide you with her maternal help and to accompany you throughout your lives. Praised be our Lord Jesus Christ!

Go out and bear fruit

I will bless the Lord at all times, his praise always on my lips (*Ps* 32:2)

1. Let us rejoice in the Lord, on this day when we contemplate another marvel of God, who in his admirable providence allows us to taste a trace of his presence in this act of self-giving Love that is the Holy Sacrifice of the Altar. ...I rejoice that, through the communications media, my words and expressions of affection can enter every house and every heart. Be sure of this: the Pope loves you, and he loves you because Jesus Christ loves you.

In this solemn eucharistic celebration, we have listened to the Gospel in which Jesus exultantly proclaims: *"I thank you, Father, Lord of heaven and earth, because you have hidden these things from the wise and understanding and revealed them to babes"* (*Mt* 11:25). I am glad that the elevation to the altars of Frei Galvão will always remain framed in the liturgy that the Church presents to us today. ...

2. Let us give thanks to God for the lasting benefits obtained through the powerful evangelizing influence that the Holy Spirit impressed upon so

many souls through Frei Galvão. The Franciscan charism, lived out in the spirit of the Gospel, has borne significant fruits through his witness as an ardent adorer of the Eucharist, as a prudent and wise guide of the souls who sought his counsel, and as a man with a great devotion to the Immaculate Conception of Mary, whose "son and perpetual servant" he considered himself to be.

God comes towards us, "he seeks to win our hearts, all the way to the Last Supper, to the piercing of his heart on the Cross, to his appearances after the Resurrection and to the great deeds by which, through the activity of the Apostles, he guided the nascent Church along its path" (Encyclical Letter *Deus Caritas Est*, 17). He reveals himself through his word, in the sacraments and especially in the Eucharist. The life of the Church, therefore, is essentially eucharistic. In his loving providence, the Lord has left us a visible sign of his presence.

When we contemplate the Lord at Mass, raised up by the priest after the consecration of the bread and wine, or when we devoutly adore him exposed in the monstrance, we renew our faith with profound humility, as Frei Galvão did in *"laus perennis"*, in a constant attitude of adoration. The Holy Eucharist contains all the spiritual wealth of the Church, that is to say Christ himself, our Passover, the living bread

come down from heaven, given life by the Holy
Spirit and in turn life-giving because it is the source
of Life for mankind. This mysterious and ineffable
manifestation of God's love for humanity occupies a
privileged place in the heart of Christians. They must
come to know the faith of the Church through her
ordained ministers, through the exemplary manner in
which they carry out the prescribed rites that always
point to the eucharistic liturgy as the centre of the
entire task of evangelization. The faithful, in their
turn, must seek to receive and to venerate the Most
Holy Sacrament with piety and devotion, eager to
welcome the Lord Jesus with faith, and having
recourse, whenever necessary, to the sacrament of
reconciliation so as to purify the soul from every
grave sin.

3. The significance of Frei Galvão's example lies in
his willingness to be of service to the people
whenever he was asked. He was renowned as a
counsellor, he was a bringer of peace to souls and
families, and a dispenser of charity especially towards
the poor and the sick. He was greatly sought out as a
confessor, because he was zealous, wise and prudent.
It is characteristic of those who truly love that they do
not want the Beloved to be offended; the conversion
of sinners was therefore the great passion of our

saint. Sister Helena Maria, the first religious sister destined to belong to the *Recolhimento de Nossa Senhora da Conceição*, witnessed to what Frei Galvão had said to her: *"Pray that the Lord our God will raise sinners with his mighty arm from the wretched depths of the sins in which they find themselves."* May this insightful admonition serve as a stimulus to us to recognize in the Divine Mercy the path towards reconciliation with God and our neighbour, for the peace of our consciences.

4. United with the Lord in the supreme communion of the Eucharist and reconciled with him and our neighbour, we will thus become bearers of that peace which the world cannot give. Will the men and women of this world be able to find peace if they are not aware of the need to be reconciled with God, with their neighbour and with themselves? Highly significant in this regard are the words written by the Assembly of the Senate of São Paulo to the Minister Provincial of the Franciscans at the end of the eighteenth century, describing Frei Galvão as a "man of peace and charity". What does the Lord ask of us? *"Love one another as I have loved you."* But immediately afterwards he adds: *"Go out and bear fruit, fruit that will last"* (cf. *Jn* 15:12,16). And what fruit does he ask of us, if not that of knowing how to

love, drawing inspiration from the example of the Saint of Guaratinguetá?

The renown of his immense charity knew no bounds. People from all over the country went to Frei Galvão, who offered a fatherly welcome to everyone. Among those who came to implore his help were the poor and the sick in body and spirit.

Jesus opens his heart and reveals to us the core of his entire saving message: *"No one has greater love than this: to lay down his life for his friends"* (*Jn* 15:13). He himself loved even to the extent of giving his life for us on the Cross. The action of the Church and of Christians in society must have this same inspiration. Pastoral initiatives for the building up of society, if directed towards the good of the poor and the sick, bear within themselves this divine seal. The Lord counts on us and calls us his friends, because it is only to those we love in this way that we are capable of giving the life offered by Jesus through his grace.

As we know, the Fifth General Conference of the Latin-American Episcopate will take as its fundamental theme: *"Disciples and Missionaries of Jesus Christ, so that our Peoples may have Life in Him"*. How can we fail to see, then, the need to listen with renewed fervour to God's call, so as to be able to respond generously to the challenges facing the Church in Brazil and in Latin America?

5. *"Come to me, all who labour and are heavy laden, and I will give you rest"*, says the Lord in the Gospel (*Mt* 11:28). This is the final recommendation that he makes to us. How can we fail to recognize here God's fatherly and at the same time motherly care towards all his children? Mary, Mother of God and our Mother, stands particularly close to us at this moment. Frei Galvão prophetically affirmed the truth of the *Immaculate Conception*. She, the *Tota Pulchra*, the Virgin Most Pure, who conceived in her womb the Redeemer of mankind and was preserved from all stain of original sin, wishes to be the definitive seal of our encounter with God our Saviour. There is no fruit of grace in the history of salvation that does not have as its necessary instrument the mediation of Our Lady.

In fact, the saint that we are celebrating gave himself irrevocably to the Mother of Jesus from his youth, desiring to belong to her for ever and he chose the Virgin Mary to be the Mother and Protector of his spiritual daughters.

My dearest friends, what a fine example Frei Galvão has left for us to follow! There is a phrase included in the formula of his consecration which sounds remarkably contemporary to us, who live in an age so full of hedonism: *"Take away my life before I offend your blessed Son, my Lord!"* They are strong words, the words of an impassioned soul, words that should be part of the normal life of every Christian, whether consecrated or not, and they enkindle a desire for fidelity to God in married couples as well as in the unmarried. The world needs transparent lives, clear souls, pure minds that refuse to be perceived as mere objects of pleasure. It is necessary to oppose those elements of the media that ridicule the sanctity of marriage and virginity before marriage.

In our day, Our Lady has been given to us as the best defence against the evils that afflict modern life; Marian devotion is the sure guarantee of her maternal protection and safeguard in the hour of temptation. And what an unfailing support is this mysterious presence of the Virgin Most Pure, when we invoke the protection and the help of the *Senhora Aparecida!* Let us place in her most holy hands the lives of priests and consecrated laypersons, seminarians and all who are called to religious life.

6. My dear friends, allow me to finish by recalling the Vigil of Prayer at Marienfeld in Germany: in the presence of a multitude of young people, I spoke of the saints of our epoch as true reformers. And I added: "Only from the saints, only from God does true revolution come, the definitive way to change the

world" (*Homily*, 20 August 2005). This is the invitation that I address to all of you today, from the first to the last, in this Eucharist without frontiers. God said: *"Be holy, as I am holy"* (*Lev* 11:44). Let us give thanks to God the Father, to God the Son, to God the Holy Spirit from whom, through the intercession of the Virgin Mary, we receive all the blessings of heaven; from whom we receive this gift which, together with faith, is the greatest grace that can be bestowed upon a creature: the firm desire to attain the fullness of charity, in the conviction that holiness is not only possible but also necessary for every person in his or her own state of life, so as to reveal to the world the true face of Christ, our friend! Amen!

Proclaim the truth of our faith

"Although he was the Son of God, he learned obedience through what he suffered; and being made perfect, he became the source of eternal salvation to all who obey him." (cf. *Heb* 5:8-9).

1. The text we have just heard in the Lesson for Vespers contains a profound teaching. Once again we realize that God's word is living and active, sharper than any two-edged sword; it penetrates to the depths of the soul and it grants solace and inspiration to his faithful servants (cf. *Heb* 4:12).

2. That is why I wished to speak first to you, the Bishops of Brazil, evoking these words, so rich in content, from the Letter to the Hebrews: *Although he was Son, he learned obedience through what he suffered; and being made perfect he became the source of eternal salvation to all who obey him"* (*Heb* 5:8-9). Filled with meaning, these verses speak of God's compassion for us, as expressed in the passion of his Son. They speak of Christ's obedience and his free, conscious acceptance of the Father's plan, which appears most clearly in his prayer on the Mount of Olives: "Not my will, but yours, be done" (*Lk* 22:42).

Jesus himself teaches us that the true way of salvation lies in conforming our will to the will of God. This is what we pray for in the third petition of the "Our Father": that God's will be done on earth as it is in heaven, since wherever God's will reigns, there the Kingdom of God is present. Jesus attracts us by his will, his filial will, and so he leads us to salvation. By freely accepting the will of God, in union with Jesus Christ, we open the world to God's Kingdom.

Purpose of the Church

We Bishops have come together to manifest this central truth, since we are directly bound to Christ, the Good Shepherd. The mission entrusted to us as teachers of the faith consists in recalling, in the words of the Apostle of the Gentiles, that our Saviour *"desires all men to be saved and to come to the knowledge of the truth"* (*1 Tim* 2:4). This, and nothing else, is the purpose of the Church: the salvation of individual souls. For this reason the Father sent his Son, and in the Lord's own words transmitted to us in the Gospel of Saint John, *"as the Father has sent me, even so I send you"* (*Jn* 20:21). Hence the mandate to preach the Gospel: *"Go therefore and make disciples of all nations, baptizing them in the name of the Father and of the Son and of the Holy Spirit, teaching them to observe all that I have commanded you; and*

lo, I am with you always, to the close of the age" (*Mt*
28:19-20). These words are simple yet sublime; they
speak of our duty to proclaim the truth of the faith,
the urgent need for the sacramental life, and the
promise of Christ's continual assistance to his Church.
These are fundamental realities: they speak of
instructing people in the faith and in Christian
morality, and of celebrating the sacraments. Wherever
God and his will are unknown, wherever faith in
Jesus Christ and in his sacramental presence is
lacking, the essential element for the solution of
pressing social and political problems is also missing.
Fidelity to the primacy of God and of his will, known
and lived in communion with Jesus Christ, is the
essential gift that we Bishops and priests must offer to
our people (cf. *Populorum Progressio*, 21).

3. Our ministry as Bishops thus impels us to discern
God's saving will and to devise a pastoral plan
capable of training God's People to recognize and
embrace transcendent values, in fidelity to the Lord
and to the Gospel.

Seeking out the lost

Certainly the present is a difficult time for the
Church, and many of her children are experiencing
difficulty. Society is experiencing moments of

worrying disorientation. The sanctity of marriage and the family are attacked with impunity, as concessions are made to forms of pressure which have a harmful effect on legislative processes; crimes against life are justified in the name of individual freedom and rights; attacks are made on the dignity of the human person; the plague of divorce and extra-marital unions is increasingly widespread. Even more: when, within the Church herself, people start to question the value of the priestly commitment as a total entrustment to God through apostolic celibacy and as a total openness to the service of souls, and preference is given to ideological, political and even party issues, the structure of total consecration to God begins to lose its deepest meaning. How can we not be deeply saddened by this? But be confident: the Church is holy and imperishable (cf. *Eph* 5:27). As Saint Augustine said: "The Church will be shaken if its foundation is shaken; but will Christ be shaken? Since Christ cannot be shaken, the Church will remain firmly established to the end of time" (*Enarrationes in Psalmos*, 103, 2, 5: PL 37, 1353).

A particular problem which you face as Pastors is surely the issue of those Catholics who have abandoned the life of the Church. It seems clear that the principal cause of this problem is to be found in the lack of an evangelization completely centred on

Christ and his Church. Those who are most vulnerable to the aggressive proselytizing of sects – a just cause for concern – and those who are incapable of resisting the onslaught of agnosticism, relativism and secularization are generally the baptized who remain insufficiently evangelized; they are easily influenced because their faith is weak, confused, easily shaken and naive, despite their innate religiosity. In the Encyclical *Deus Caritas Est*, I stated that "being Christian is not the result of an ethical choice or a lofty idea, but the encounter with an event, a person, which gives life a new horizon and a decisive direction" (no. 1). Consequently, there is a need to engage in apostolic activity as a true mission in the midst of the flock that is constituted by the Catholic Church in Brazil, and to promote on every level a methodical evangelization aimed at personal and communal fidelity to Christ. *No effort should be spared in seeking out those Catholics who have fallen away and those who know little or nothing of Jesus Christ*, by implementing a pastoral plan which welcomes them and helps them realize that the Church is a privileged place of encounter with God, and also through a continuing process of catechesis.

What is required, in a word, is a mission of evangelization capable of engaging all the vital

energies present in this immense flock. My thoughts
turn to the priests, the men and women religious
and the laity who work so generously, often in the
face of immense difficulties, in order to spread the
truth of the Gospel. Many of them cooperate with
or actively participate in the associations,
movements and other new ecclesial realities that, in
communion with the Pastors and in harmony with
diocesan guidelines, bring their spiritual,
educational and missionary richness to the heart of
the Church, as a precious experience and a model
of Christian life.

In this work of evangelization the ecclesial
community should be clearly marked by pastoral
initiatives, especially by sending missionaries, lay or
religious, to homes on the outskirts of the cities and
in the interior, to enter into dialogue with everyone
in a spirit of understanding, sensitivity and charity.
On the other hand, if the persons they encounter are
living in poverty, it is necessary to help them, as the
first Christian communities did, by practising
solidarity and making them feel truly loved. The poor
living in the outskirts of the cities or the countryside
need to feel that the Church is close to them,
providing for their most urgent needs, defending
their rights and working together with them to build
a society founded on justice and peace. The Gospel

is addressed in a special way to the poor, and the Bishop, modelled on the Good Shepherd, must be particularly concerned with offering them the divine consolation of the faith, without overlooking their need for "material bread". As I wished to stress in the Encyclical *Deus Caritas Est*, "the Church cannot neglect the service of charity any more than she can neglect the sacraments and the word" (no. 22).

The sacramental life, especially in the celebration of Confession and the Eucharist, here takes on a particular importance. As Pastors, it is your primary task to ensure that the faithful share in the eucharistic life and in the Sacrament of Reconciliation. You must be vigilant to ensure that the confession and absolution of sins is ordinarily individual, inasmuch as sin itself is something profoundly personal (cf. Post-Synodal Apostolic Exhortation *Reconciliatio et Paenitentia*, 31, III). Only physical or moral impossibility exempts the faithful from this form of confession, in which case reconciliation can be obtained by some other means (cf. *Code of Canon Law*, can. 960, *Compendium of the Catechism of the Catholic Church*, 311). It is appropriate, therefore, to instil in priests the practice of generously making themselves available to the faithful who have recourse to the sacrament of God's mercy (cf. Apostolic Letter *Misericordia Dei*, 2).

Catechesis and Liturgy

4. Starting afresh from Christ in every area of missionary activity; rediscovering in Jesus the love and salvation given to us by the Father through the Holy Spirit: this is the substance and lifeline of the episcopal mission which makes the Bishop the person primarily responsible for catechesis in his diocese. Indeed, it falls ultimately to him to direct catechesis, surrounding himself with competent and trustworthy co-workers. *It is therefore clear that the catechist's task is not simply to communicate faith-experiences; rather – under the guidance of the Pastor – it is to be an authentic herald of revealed truths.* Faith is a journey led by the Holy Spirit which can be summed up in two words: conversion and discipleship. In the Christian tradition, these two key words clearly indicate that faith in Christ implies a way of living based on the twofold command to love God and neighbour – and they also express life's social dimension.

Truth presupposes a clear understanding of Jesus' message transmitted by means of an intelligible, inculturated language, which must nevertheless remain faithful to the Gospel's intent. At this time, there is an urgent need for an adequate knowledge of the faith as it is presented in the *Catechism of the Catholic Church* and its accompanying *Compendium*. Education in Christian personal and social virtues is also an essential part of catechesis, as is education in social responsibility. Precisely because faith, life, and the celebration of the sacred liturgy – the source of faith and life – are inseparable, there is need for a more correct implementation of the liturgical principles as indicated by the Second Vatican Council, as well as those contained in the *Directory for the Pastoral Ministry of Bishops* (cf. 145-151), so as to restore to the liturgy its sacred character. It was with this end in view that my Venerable Predecessor on the Chair of Peter, John Paul II, wished "to appeal urgently that the liturgical norms for the celebration of the Eucharist be observed with great fidelity ... Liturgy is never anyone's private property, be it of the celebrant or of the community in which the mysteries are celebrated" (Encyclical Letter *Ecclesia de Eucharistia*, 52). For Bishops, who are the "moderators of the Church's liturgical life", the rediscovery and appreciation of obedience to liturgical norms is a form of witness to the one, universal Church, that presides in charity.

Important duties

5. A leap forward in the quality of people's Christian lives is needed, so that they can bear witness to their faith in a clear and transparent way. This faith, as it is celebrated and shared in the liturgy and in works of

charity, nourishes and reinvigorates the community of the Lord's disciples while building them up as the missionary and prophetic Church. The Brazilian Episcopate has an impressive structure based on recently revised and more easily implemented statutes which focus more directly on the good of the Church. The Pope has come to Brazil to ask that, through following the word of God, all these Venerable Brothers in the Episcopate truly become messengers of *eternal salvation for all those who obey Christ* (cf. *Heb* 5:9). If we are to stay true to our solemn commitment as successors of the Apostles, we Pastors must be faithful servants of the word, eschewing any reductive or mistaken vision of the mission entrusted to us. It is not enough to look at reality solely from the viewpoint of personal faith; we must work with the Gospel in our hands and anchor ourselves in the authentic heritage of the Apostolic Tradition, free from any interpretations motivated by rationalistic ideologies.

Indeed, "within the particular Churches, it is the Bishop's responsibility to guard and interpret the word of God and to make authoritative judgments as to what is or is not in conformity with it" (Congregation for the Doctrine of the Faith, *Instruction on the Ecclesial Vocation of the Theologian*, 19). As the primary Teacher of faith and doctrine, the Bishop will rely on collaboration with the theologian, who, in order "to be faithful to his role of service to the truth, must take into account the proper mission of the Magisterium and collaborate with it" (*ibid.*, 20). The duty to preserve the deposit of faith and safeguard its unity calls for strict vigilance so that the faith may be "preserved and handed down with fidelity and so that particular insights are clearly integrated into the one Gospel of Christ" (*Directory for the Pastoral Ministry of Bishops*, 126).

This, therefore, is the enormous responsibility you have assumed as formators of your people, and especially of the priests and religious under your care. They are you faithful co-workers. I am aware of your commitment to seeking ways of forming new vocations to the priesthood and religious life. Theological formation, as well as education in sacred sciences, needs to be constantly updated, but this must always be done in accord with the Church's authentic Magisterium.

I appeal to your priestly zeal and your sense of vocational discernment, especially so that you will know how to bring to completion the spiritual, psychological and affective, intellectual and pastoral formation needed to prepare young people for mature, generous service to the Church. Good and assiduous spiritual direction is indispensable for fostering human growth and eliminating the risk of going astray in the area of sexuality. Always keep in mind that priestly celibacy "is a gift which the Church has received and desires to retain, convinced that it is a good for the Church itself and for the world" (*Directory on the Ministry and Life of Priests*, 57).

I would also like to commend to your care the religious communities which play such an important role in the lives of your dioceses. They offer their own valuable contribution since "there are varieties of gifts, but the same Spirit" (*1 Cor* 12:4). The Church cannot help but show its joy and gratitude for all that religious men and women are able to contribute in universities, schools, hospitals, and other works and institutions.

One faith one baptism

6. I am familiar with the dynamic of your Assemblies and the efforts involved in formulating the various pastoral plans so that they give priority to the formation of clergy and those who assist them in their pastoral work. Some of you have encouraged evangelization movements to assist in the work of gathering groups of faithful together to carry out certain types of action. The Successor of Peter is relying on you to ensure that the preparation you give them is always based on a spirituality of

communion and fidelity to the See of Peter, so that the work of the Spirit is never in vain. In fact, *the integrity of the faith, together with ecclesiastical discipline, is and will always be an area requiring careful oversight on your part, especially when it comes to living out the consequences of the fact that "there is only one faith and one baptism".*

As you know, among the various documents dealing with Christian unity, there is the *Directory for Ecumenism* published by the Pontifical Council for Promoting Christian Unity. Ecumenism – or the search for unity among Christians – has become in our time an increasingly urgent task for the Catholic Church, as is evident from the growth of intercultural exchange and the challenge of secularism. Consequently, given the rapidly growing number of new Christian denominations, and especially certain forms of often aggressive proselytism, the work of ecumenism has become more complex. In this context, a good historical and doctrinal formation is absolutely essential, so as to foster necessary discernment and lead to a better understanding of the specific identity of each of these communities, the elements that divide them, and those elements that can be helpful on the road to greater unity. The greatest area of common ground for collaboration should be the defence of fundamental moral values –

transmitted by the biblical tradition – against the
relativistic and consumerist cultural forces that seek
to destroy them. Another such area is faith in God
the Creator and in Jesus Christ his incarnate Son.
Moreover, there will always be the principle of
fraternal love and the search for mutual
understanding and *rapprochement*. Yet we must also
be concerned with defending the faith of our people,
confirming them in the joyful certitude that *"unica
Christi Ecclesia...subsistit in Ecclesia catholica, a
successore Petri et Episcopis in eius communione
gubernata"* ["The one Church of Christ...subsists in
the Catholic Church which is governed by the
successor of Peter and by the Bishops in communion
with him"] (*Lumen Gentium*, 8).

In this way, through the National Council of
Christian Churches, you will be able to move towards
candid ecumenical dialogue, committing yourselves
to complete respect for those other religious
confessions that wish to remain in contact with the
Catholic Church in Brazil.

7. There is nothing new in the observation that your
country is living through a historic deficit in social
development, whose extreme effects can seen in the
vast cross-section of Brazilians living in need and the
great inequalities in income, even at the highest
levels of society. It is your task, my dear Brothers, as

the hierarchy of the people of God, to promote the search for new solutions imbued with the Christian spirit. A vision of the economy and social problems from the perspective of the Church's social teaching should always bring us to consider things from the viewpoint of human dignity, which transcends the simple interplay of economic factors. Hence, it is necessary to work untiringly to form politicians, and all Brazilians who wield a certain influence, be it great or small, as well as all members of society, so that they can fully assume their responsibilities and learn to give the economy a truly human and compassionate face.

There is a need to form a genuine spirit of truthfulness and honesty among the political and commercial classes. Those who take on leadership roles in society must try to foresee the social consequences – direct and indirect, short-term and long-term – of their own decisions, always acting according to the criteria that will maximize the common good, rather than merely seeking personal profit. ...

Hope does not disappoint

Be praised, my Lord, for all your creatures!

With these words, addressed to the Almighty and Good Lord, the Poor Saint of Assisi acknowledged the unique bounty of God the Creator, and the tenderness, strength and beauty that gently flows out upon all his creatures, making them mirrors of the Creator's omnipotence.

Dear Sisters, spiritual daughters of Saint Clare, our gathering here in this "Fazenda da Esperança" is meant to be a sign of the affection of the Successor of Peter towards the cloistered Sisters, and also a serene manifestation of love, echoing through the hills and valleys of the Mantiqueira mountain-range and spreading throughout the whole land: "No speech, no word, no voice is heard; yet their span extends through all the earth, their words to the utmost bounds of the world" (*Ps* 18:4-5). From this place, the daughters of Saint Clare proclaim: *"Be praised, my Lord, for all your creatures!"*

In places where society no longer sees any future or hope, Christians are called to proclaim the power of the Resurrection: it is here, in this "Fazenda da

Esperança" – home to so many, especially young people, who are seeking to overcome drug addiction, alcoholism, and chemical dependency – that a clear witness is given to the Gospel of Christ amid a consumer society far removed from God. What a contrast from the prospect of the Creator beholding his work! In their contemplative lives, the Poor Clare Sisters and other cloistered religious gaze upon the greatness of God and also discover the beauty of his creation; hence they can picture him as the sacred author indicates, caught up in wonder at his handiwork, his beloved creation: "And God saw everything that he had made, and behold, it was very good!" (*Gen* 1:31).

When sin entered the world, and with sin, death, God's beloved creation, though wounded, was not totally deprived of beauty: on the contrary, a still greater love was received: "O happy fault, which gained for us so great a Redeemer!" – as the Church proclaims in the *Exsultet* during the mysterious and radiant night of Easter. It is the risen Christ who heals the wounds and saves the sons and daughters of God, saves humanity from death, from sin and from slavery to passions. The Passover of Christ unites heaven and earth. In this "Fazenda da Esperança", the prayers of the Poor Clare Sisters are united with the demanding work of medicine and therapy in order to vanquish the prisons and break the chains of drugs that bring so much suffering to God's beloved children.

In this way God's creation is restored to the beauty that so delights and amazes its Creator. He is the Almighty Father, it is he alone whose essence is love and whose glory is man fully alive, in the expression of Saint Irenaeus. He "so loved the world that he gave his only Son" (*Jn* 3:16), in order to raise up the one who had fallen along the roadside, attacked and wounded by thieves on the way from Jerusalem to Jericho. On the pathways of the world, Jesus is "the hand" that the Father stretches out to sinners; he is the way that leads to peace (cf. *Second Eucharistic Prayer for Reconciliation*). Truly we discover here that the beauty of creation and the love of God are inseparable. Francis and Clare of Assisi also discover this secret and they propose to their beloved sons and daughters one very simple thing: to live the Gospel. This is their norm of conduct and their rule of life. Clare expressed it very well when she said to her sisters: "Among yourselves, my daughters, let there be the same love with which Christ has loved you" (*Testament of St Clare*).

In this same love, Brother Hans invited them to be the guarantors of all the work carried out in the "Fazenda da Esperança". Through the strength of silent prayer, through fasting and penance, the daughters of Saint Clare live out the commandment of love for God and neighbour in its supreme form, loving to the end.

This means that we must never lose hope! Hence the name given to this work by Brother Hans: "Fazenda da Esperança". We need to build up hope, weaving the fabric of a society that, by relaxing its grip on the threads of life, is losing the true sense of hope. This loss, according to Saint Paul, is the self-imposed curse of "heartless persons" (cf. *Rom* 1:31).

My dear Sisters, make it your task to proclaim that "hope does not disappoint" (*Rom* 5:5). May the sorrow of the Crucified Lord, which filled Mary's soul at the foot of the Cross, console the hearts of many mothers and fathers who weep with sorrow because of their children's continuing dependency on drugs. By your silent prayerful self-offering, an eloquent silence that the Father hears, proclaim the message of love that conquers sorrow, drugs and death. Proclaim Jesus Christ, a human being like us, who suffers like ourselves, who took our sins upon himself in order to deliver us from them! ...

Be open to the desire for God

At last I am here with you at "Fazenda da Esperança"!

1. I greet with particular affection Brother Hans Stapel, founder of the charity "Nossa Senhora da Glória", which is also known as "Fazenda da Esperança". Firstly I wish to rejoice with each of you for having believed in the ideals of good and of peace which define this place.

To all of you who have come here today from the various "fazendas" to be with the Pope – those undergoing treatment and those who have been cured, volunteers, families, those who have already been through the programme, and benefactors – I wish to say: *pax et bonum!*

I know that there are representatives here from other places where the "Fazenda da Esperança" has opened centres. You have come to see the Pope. You have come to listen and to assimilate what I wish to say to you.

2. The Church of today needs a renewed awareness of its task to draw the world's attention to the voice of him who says: *"I am the light of the world; he who*

follows me will not walk in darkness, but will have the light of life" (*Jn* 8:12). It is the Pope's mission to renew in the hearts of people everywhere that light which does not grow dim, because it seeks to illumine the depths of every soul that seeks the true good and peace that the world cannot give. All that this light needs is a heart open to the desire for God. God does not force us, he does not oppress our individual freedom; he simply asks for openness in the inner sanctum of our conscience, through which pass all our noblest aspirations, as well as the affections and disordered passions which tend to obscure the message of the Almighty.

3. *"Behold, I stand at the door and knock; if anyone hears my voice and opens the door, I will come in to him and eat with him, and he with me"* (*Rev* 3:20). These are divine words which penetrate to the depths of our souls and shake us at our deepest roots.

At some stage in people's lives, Jesus comes and gently knocks at the hearts of those properly disposed. Perhaps for you, he did this through a friend or a priest, or, who knows, perhaps he arranged a series of coincidences which enabled you to realize that you are loved by God. Through the institution which has welcomed you, the Lord has given you this opportunity for physical and spiritual recovery, so vital for you and your families. In turn, society expects you to spread this precious gift of health among your friends and all the members of the community.

You must be Ambassadors of hope! Brazil's statistics concerning drug abuse and other forms of chemical dependency are very high. The same is true of Latin America in general. I therefore urge the drug-dealers to reflect on the grave harm they are inflicting on countless young people and on adults from every level of society: God will call you to account for your deeds. Human dignity cannot be trampled upon in this way. The harm done will receive the same censure that Jesus reserved for those who gave scandal to the "little ones", the favourites of God (cf. *Mt* 18:7-10).

4. Through treatment, which includes medical, psychological and educational assistance, and through much prayer, manual work and discipline, many people – especially young people – have already succeeded in freeing themselves from alcohol and drug dependency, thereby recovering meaning in their lives.

I wish to express my appreciation for this work, which has the charism of Saint Francis and the spirituality of the Focolare Movement as its spiritual foundation.

Reintegration in society undoubtedly demonstrates the effectiveness of your initiative. Yet it is the conversions, the rediscovery of God and active participation in the life of the Church which attract even greater attention and which confirm the importance of your work. It is not enough to care for the body, we must adorn the soul with the most precious divine gifts acquired through Baptism.

Let us thank God for all those who have set out along the path of renewed hope, with the help of the Sacrament of Reconciliation and the celebration of the Eucharist.

5. Dear friends, I cannot let this opportunity pass without thanking all those who contribute materially and spiritually to enable the charity "Nossa Senhora da Glória" to continue its work. May God bless Brother Hans Stapel and Nelson Giovanelli Ros for having answered his call to devote their lives to you. I ask the Lord also to bless all those who work here: the consecrated men and women, and the volunteers. We ask God's special blessing too on all those friends, support groups and authorities who supply your needs, and on all those who love Christ present in these beloved children of his.

My thoughts turn now to those many other institutions throughout the world which work to rebuild and renew the lives of these brothers and sisters of ours present in our midst, whom God loves with a preferential love. I am thinking of groups such as Alcoholics Anonymous and Narcotics Anonymous as well as the sobriety associations working generously in many communities so as to build up the lives of others.

6. The proximity of the Shrine of Aparecida assures us that the "Fazenda da Esperança" came into being under her protection and maternal gaze. For a long time now, in my prayers, I have been asking Our Lady, Queen and Patron of Brazil, to extend her protective mantle over the participants in the Fifth General Conference of the Bishops of Latin America and the Caribbean. Your presence here provides a considerable help for the success of this great gathering; offer your prayers, sacrifices, and renunciations on the altar of the Chapel, in the certainty that they will rise up to heaven in the Holy Sacrifice of the Mass as a fragrant offering to Almighty God. I am counting on your help! May Saint Frei Galvão and Saint Crescentia keep watch over you and protect each one of you. I bless you all in the name of the Father and of the Son and of the Holy Spirit. Amen.

Being disciples of Christ today

1. The Christian faith in Latin America

Faith in God has animated the life and culture of these nations for more than five centuries. From the encounter between that faith and the indigenous peoples, there has emerged the rich Christian culture of this Continent, expressed in art, music, literature, and above all, in the religious traditions and in the peoples' whole way of being, united as they are by a shared history and a shared creed that give rise to a great underlying harmony, despite the diversity of cultures and languages. At present, this same faith has some serious challenges to address, because the harmonious development of society and the Catholic identity of these peoples are in jeopardy. In this regard, the Fifth General Conference is preparing to reflect upon this situation, in order to help the Christian faithful to live their faith with joy and coherence, to deepen their awareness of being disciples and missionaries of Christ, sent by him into the world to proclaim and to bear witness to our faith and love.

Yet what did the acceptance of the Christian faith mean for the nations of Latin America and the Caribbean? For them, it meant knowing and welcoming

Christ, the unknown God whom their ancestors were seeking, without realizing it, in their rich religious traditions. Christ is the Saviour for whom they were silently longing. It also meant that they received, in the waters of Baptism, the divine life that made them children of God by adoption; moreover, they received the Holy Spirit who came to make their cultures fruitful, purifying them and developing the numerous seeds that the incarnate Word had planted in them, thereby guiding them along the paths of the Gospel. In effect, the proclamation of Jesus and of his Gospel did not at any point involve an alienation of the pre-Columbian cultures, nor was it the imposition of a foreign culture. Authentic cultures are not closed in upon themselves, nor are they set in stone at a particular point in history, but they are open, or better still, they are seeking an encounter with other cultures, hoping to reach universality through encounter and dialogue with other ways of life and with elements that can lead to a new synthesis, in which the diversity of expressions is always respected as well as the diversity of their particular cultural embodiment.

Ultimately, it is only the truth that can bring unity, and the proof of this is love. That is why Christ, being in truth the incarnate *Logos*, "love to the end", is not alien to any culture, nor to any person; on the contrary, the response that he seeks in the heart of cultures is what gives them their ultimate identity, uniting humanity and at the same time respecting the wealth of diversity, opening people everywhere to growth in genuine humanity, in authentic progress. The Word of God, in becoming flesh in Jesus Christ, also became history and culture.

The Utopia of going back to breathe life into the pre-Columbian religions, separating them from Christ and from the universal Church, would not be a step forward: indeed, it would be a step back. In reality, it would be a retreat towards a stage in history anchored in the past.

The wisdom of the indigenous peoples fortunately led them to form a synthesis between their cultures and the Christian faith which the missionaries were offering them. Hence the rich and profound popular religiosity, in which we see the soul of the Latin American peoples:

• love for the suffering Christ, the God of compassion, pardon and reconciliation; the God who loved us to the point of handing himself over for us;

• love for the Lord present in the Eucharist, the incarnate God, dead and risen in order to be the bread of life; the God who is close to the poor and to those who suffer;

• the profound devotion to the most holy Virgin of Guadalupe, the *Aparecida*, the Virgin invoked under various national and local titles. When the Virgin of Guadalupe appeared to the native Indian Saint Juan Diego, she spoke these important words to him: *"Am I not your mother? Are you not under my shadow and my gaze? Am I not the source of your joy? Are you not sheltered underneath my mantle, under the embrace of my arms?"* (Nican Mopohua, nos. 118-119).

This religiosity is also expressed in devotion to the saints with their patronal feasts, in love for the Pope and the other Pastors, and in love for the universal Church as the great family of God, that neither can nor ever should leave her children alone or destitute. All this forms the great mosaic of popular piety which is the precious treasure of the Catholic Church in Latin America, and must be protected, promoted and, when necessary, purified.

2. Continuity with the other Conferences

This Fifth General Conference is being celebrated in continuity with the other four that preceded it: in Rio de Janeiro, Medellín, Puebla and Santo Domingo. With the same spirit that was at work there, the Bishops now wish to give a new impetus to evangelization, so that these peoples may continue to grow and mature in their faith in order to be the light of the world and witnesses to Jesus Christ with their own lives.

After the Fourth General Conference, in Santo Domingo, many changes took place in society. The Church which shares in the achievements and the hopes, the sufferings and the joys of her children, wishes to walk alongside them at this challenging time, so as to inspire them always with hope and comfort (cf. *Gaudium et Spes*, 1).

Today's world experiences the phenomenon of globalization as a network of relationships extending over the whole planet. Although from certain points of view this benefits the great family of humanity, and is a sign of its profound aspiration towards unity, nevertheless it also undoubtedly brings with it the risk of vast monopolies and of treating profit as the supreme value. As in all areas of human activity, globalization too must be led by ethics, placing everything at the service of the human person, created in the image and likeness of God.

In Latin America and the Caribbean, as well as in other regions, there has been notable progress towards democracy, although there are grounds for concern in the face of authoritarian forms of government and regimes wedded to certain ideologies that we thought had been superseded, and which do not correspond to the Christian vision of man and society as taught by the Social Doctrine of the Church. On the other side of the coin, the liberal economy of some Latin American countries must take account of equity, because of the ever increasing sectors of society that find themselves oppressed by immense poverty or even despoiled of their own natural resources.

In the ecclesial communities of Latin America there is a notable degree of maturity in faith among the many active lay men and women devoted to the Lord, and there are also many generous catechists, many young people, new ecclesial movements and recently established Institutes of consecrated life. Many Catholic educational, charitable or housing initiatives have proved essential. Yet it is true that one can detect a certain weakening of Christian life in society overall and of participation in the life of the Catholic Church, due to secularism, hedonism, indifferentism and proselytism by numerous sects, animist religions and new pseudo-religious phenomena.

All of this constitutes a new situation which will be analyzed here at Aparecida. Faced with new and difficult choices, the faithful are looking to this Fifth Conference for renewal and revitalization of their faith in Christ, our one Teacher and Saviour, who has revealed to us the unique experience of the infinite love of God the Father for mankind. From this source, new paths and creative pastoral plans will be able to emerge, capable of instilling a firm hope for living out the faith joyfully and responsibly, and thus spreading it in one's own surroundings.

3. Disciples and Missionaries

This General Conference has as its theme: "Disciples and Missionaries of Jesus Christ, so that our peoples may have life in him".

The Church has the great task of guarding and nourishing the faith of the People of God, and reminding the faithful of this Continent that, by virtue of their Baptism, they are called to be disciples and missionaries of Jesus Christ. This implies following him, living in intimacy with him, imitating his example and bearing witness. Every baptized person receives from Christ, like the Apostles, the missionary mandate: *"Go into all the world and preach the Gospel to the whole creation. Whoever believes and is baptized, will be saved"* (*Mk* 16:15). To be disciples and missionaries of Jesus Christ and to seek life "in him" presupposes being deeply rooted in him.

What does Christ actually give us? Why do we want to be disciples of Christ? The answer is: because, in communion with him, we hope to find life, the true life that is worthy of the name, and thus

we want to make him known to others, to
communicate to them the gift that we have found in
him. But is it really so? Are we really convinced that
Christ is the way, the truth and the life?

In the face of the priority of faith in Christ and of
life "in him", formulated in the title of this Fifth
Conference, a further question could arise: could this
priority not perhaps be a flight towards
emotionalism, towards religious individualism, an
abandonment of the urgent reality of the great
economic, social and political problems of Latin
America and the world, and a flight from reality
towards a spiritual world?

As a first step, we can respond to this question
with another: what is this "reality"? What is real? Are
only material goods, social, economic and political
problems "reality"? This was precisely the great error
of the dominant tendencies of the last century, a
most destructive error, as we can see from the results
of both Marxist and capitalist systems. They falsify
the notion of reality by detaching it from the
foundational and decisive reality which is God.
Anyone who excludes God from his horizons falsifies
the notion of "reality" and, in consequence, can only
end up in blind alleys or with recipes for destruction.

The first basic point to affirm, then, is the
following: only those who recognize God know

reality and are able to respond to it adequately and in a truly human manner. The truth of this thesis becomes evident in the face of the collapse of all the systems that marginalize God.

Yet here a further question immediately arises: who knows God? How can we know him? We cannot enter here into a complex discussion of this fundamental issue. For a Christian, the nucleus of the reply is simple: only God knows God, only his Son who is God from God, true God, knows him. And he "who is nearest to the Father's heart has made him known" (*Jn* 1:18). Hence the unique and irreplaceable importance of Christ for us, for humanity. If we do not know God in and with Christ, all of reality is transformed into an indecipherable enigma; there is no way, and without a way, there is neither life nor truth.

God is the foundational reality, not a God who is merely imagined or hypothetical, but God with a human face; he is God-with-us, the God who loves even to the Cross. When the disciple arrives at an understanding of this love of Christ "to the end", he cannot fail to respond to this love with a similar love: "I will follow you wherever you go" (*Lk* 9:57).

We can ask ourselves a further question: what does faith in this God give us? The first response is: it gives us a family, the universal family of God in the

Catholic Church. Faith releases us from the isolation of the "I", because it leads us to communion: the encounter with God is, in itself and as such, an encounter with our brothers and sisters, an act of convocation, of unification, of responsibility towards the other and towards others. In this sense, the preferential option for the poor is implicit in the Christological faith in the God who became poor for us, so as to enrich us with his poverty (cf. *2 Cor* 8:9).

Yet before we consider what is entailed by the realism of our faith in the God who became man, we must explore the question more deeply: how can we truly know Christ so as to be able to follow him and live with him, so as to find life in him and to communicate that life to others, to society and to the world? First and foremost, Christ makes his person, his life and his teaching known to us through the word of God. At the beginning of this new phase that the missionary Church of Latin America and the Caribbean is preparing to enter, starting with this Fifth General Conference in Aparecida, an indispensable pre-condition is profound knowledge of the word of God.

To achieve this, we must train people to read and meditate on the word of God: this must become their staple diet, so that, through their own experience, the faithful will see that the words of Jesus are spirit and life (cf. *Jn* 6:63). Otherwise, how could they proclaim a message whose content and spirit they do not know thoroughly? We must build our missionary commitment and the whole of our lives on the rock of the word of God. For this reason, I encourage the Bishops to strive to make it known.

An important way of introducing the People of God to the mystery of Christ is through *catechesis*. Here, the message of Christ is transmitted in a simple and substantial form. It is therefore necessary to intensify the catechesis and the faith formation not only of children but also of young people and adults. Mature reflection on faith is a light for the path of life and a source of strength for witnessing to Christ. Most valuable tools with which to achieve this are the *Catechism of the Catholic Church* and its abridged version, the *Compendium of the Catechism of the Catholic Church*.

In this area, we must not limit ourselves solely to homilies, lectures, Bible courses or theology courses, but we must have recourse also to the communications media: press, radio and television, websites, forums and many other methods for effectively communicating the message of Christ to a large number of people.

In this effort to come to know the message of Christ and to make it a guide for our own lives, we must remember that evangelization has always developed alongside the promotion of the human person and authentic Christian liberation. "Love of God and love of neighbour have become one; in the least of the brethren we find Jesus himself, and in Jesus we find God" (Encyclical Letter *Deus Caritas Est*, 15). For the same reason, there will also need to be social catechesis and a sufficient formation in the social teaching of the Church, for which a very useful tool is the *Compendium of the Social Doctrine of the Church*. The Christian life is not expressed solely in personal virtues, but also in social and political virtues.

The disciple, founded in this way upon the rock of God's word, feels driven to bring the Good News of salvation to his brothers and sisters. *Discipleship and mission* are like the two sides of a single coin: when the disciple is in love with Christ, he cannot stop proclaiming to the world that only in him do we find salvation (cf. *Acts* 4:12). In effect, the disciple knows that without Christ there is no light, no hope, no love, no future.

4. "So that in him they may have life"

The peoples of Latin America and the Caribbean have the right to a full life, proper to the children of God, under conditions that are more human: free from the threat of hunger and from every form of violence. For these peoples, their Bishops must promote a culture of life which can permit, in the words of my predecessor Paul VI, "the passage from misery towards the possession of necessities ... the acquisition of culture ... cooperation for the common good ... the acknowledgement by man of supreme values, and of God, their source and their finality" (*Populorum Progressio*, 21).

In this context I am pleased to recall the Encyclical *Populorum Progressio*, the fortieth anniversary of which we celebrate this year. This Papal document emphasizes that authentic development must be integral, that is, directed to the promotion of the whole person and of all people (cf. no. 14), and it invites all to overcome grave social inequalities and the enormous differences in access to goods. These peoples are yearning, above all, for the fullness of life that Christ brought us: "I came that they may have life, and have it abundantly" (*Jn* 10:10). With this divine life, human existence is likewise developed to the full, in its personal, family, social and cultural dimensions.

In order to form the disciple and sustain the missionary in his great task, the Church offers him, in addition to the bread of the word, the bread of the Eucharist. In this regard, we find inspiration and illumination in the passage from the Gospel about the disciples on the road to Emmaus. When they sit at table and receive from Jesus Christ the bread that has been blessed and broken, their eyes are opened and they discover the face of the Risen Lord, they feel in their hearts that everything he said and did was the truth, and that the redemption of the world has already begun to unfold. Every Sunday and every Eucharist is a personal encounter with Christ. Listening to God's word, our hearts burn because it is he who is explaining and proclaiming it. When we break the bread at the Eucharist, it is he whom we receive personally. The Eucharist is indispensable nourishment for the life of the disciple and missionary of Christ.

Sunday Mass, Centre of Christian life

Hence the need to give priority in pastoral programmes to appreciation of the importance of Sunday Mass. We must motivate Christians to take an active part in it, and if possible, to bring their families, which is even better. The participation of parents with their children at Sunday Mass is an effective way of teaching the faith and it is a close bond that maintains their unity with one another. Sunday, throughout the Church's life, has been the privileged moment of the community's encounter with the risen Lord.

Christians should be aware that they are not following a character from past history, but the living Christ, present in the *today* and the *now* of their lives. He is the living one who walks alongside us, revealing to us the meaning of events, of suffering and death, of rejoicing and feasting, entering our homes and remaining there, feeding us with the bread that gives life. For this reason Sunday Mass must be the centre of Christian life.

The encounter with Christ in the Eucharist calls forth a commitment to evangelization and an impulse towards solidarity; it awakens in the Christian a strong desire to proclaim the Gospel and to bear witness to it in the world so as to build a more just and humane society. From the Eucharist, in the course of the centuries, an immense wealth of charity has sprung forth, of sharing in the difficulties of others, of love and of justice. Only from the Eucharist will the civilization of love spring forth which will transform Latin America and the Caribbean, making them not only the Continent of Hope, but also the Continent of Love!

Social and Political problems

Having arrived at this point, we can ask ourselves a question: how can the Church contribute to the solution of urgent social and political problems, and

respond to the great challenge of poverty and
destitution? The problems of Latin America and the
Caribbean, like those of today's world, are
multifaceted and complex, and they cannot be dealt
with through generic programmes. Undoubtedly, the
fundamental question about the way that the Church,
illuminated by faith in Christ, should react to these
challenges, is one that concerns us all. In this
context, we inevitably speak of the problem of
structures, especially those which create injustice. In
truth, just structures are a condition without which a
just order in society is not possible. But how do they
arise? How do they function? Both capitalism and
Marxism promised to point out the path for the
creation of just structures, and they declared that
these, once established, would function by
themselves; they declared that not only would they
have no need of any prior individual morality, but
that they would promote a communal morality. And
this ideological promise has been proved false. The
facts have clearly demonstrated it. The Marxist
system, where it found its way into government, not
only left a sad heritage of economic and ecological
destruction, but also a painful oppression of souls.
And we can also see the same thing happening in
the West, where the distance between rich and poor
is growing constantly, and giving rise to a worrying

degradation of personal dignity through drugs, alcohol and deceptive illusions of happiness.

Just structures are, as I have said, an indispensable condition for a just society, but they neither arise nor function without a moral consensus in society on fundamental values, and on the need to live these values with the necessary sacrifices, even if this goes against personal interest.

Where God is absent – God with the human face of Jesus Christ – these values fail to show themselves with their full force, nor does a consensus arise concerning them. I do not mean that non-believers cannot live a lofty and exemplary morality; I am only saying that a society in which God is absent will not find the necessary consensus on moral values or the strength to live according to the model of these values, even when they are in conflict with private interests.

On the other hand, just structures must be sought and elaborated in the light of fundamental values, with the full engagement of political, economic and social reasoning. They are a question of *recta ratio* and they do not arise from ideologies nor from their premises. Certainly there exists a great wealth of political experience and expertise on social and economic problems that can highlight the fundamental elements of a just state and the paths that must be avoided. But in different cultural and political situations, amid constant developments in technology and changes in the historical reality of the world, adequate answers must be sought in a rational manner, and a consensus must be created – with the necessary commitments – on the structures that must be established.

This political task is not the immediate competence of the Church. Respect for a healthy secularity – including the pluralism of political opinions – is essential in the Christian tradition. If the Church were to start transforming herself into a directly political subject, she would do less, not more, for the poor and for justice, because she would lose her independence and her moral authority, identifying herself with a single political path and with debatable partisan positions. The Church is the advocate of justice and of the poor, precisely because she does not identify with politicians nor with partisan interests. Only by remaining independent can she teach the great criteria and inalienable values, guide consciences and offer a life choice that goes beyond the political sphere. To form consciences, to be the advocate of justice and truth, to educate in individual and political virtues: that is the fundamental vocation of the Church in this area. And lay Catholics must be aware of their responsibilities in public life; they must be present in the formation of the necessary consensus and in opposition to injustice.

Just structures will never be complete in a definitive way. As history continues to evolve, they must be constantly renewed and updated; they must always be imbued with a political and humane *ethos* – and we have to work hard to ensure its presence and effectiveness. In other words, the presence of God, friendship with the incarnate Son of God, the light of his word: these are always fundamental conditions for the presence and efficacy of justice and love in our societies.

This being a Continent of baptized Christians, it is time to overcome the notable absence – in the political sphere, in the world of the media and in the universities – of the voices and initiatives of Catholic leaders with strong personalities and generous dedication, who are coherent in their ethical and religious convictions. The ecclesial movements have plenty of room here to remind the laity of their responsibility and their mission to bring the light of the Gospel into public life, into culture, economics and politics.

5. Other priority areas

In order to bring about this renewal of the Church that has been entrusted to your care in these lands, let me draw your attention to some areas that I consider priorities for this new phase.

The family

The family, the "patrimony of humanity", constitutes one of the most important treasures of Latin American countries. The family was and is the school of faith, the training-ground for human and civil values, the hearth in which human life is born and is generously and responsibly welcomed. Undoubtedly, it is currently suffering a degree of adversity caused by secularism and by ethical relativism, by movements of population internally and externally, by poverty, by social instability and by civil legislation opposed to marriage which, by supporting contraception and abortion, is threatening the future of peoples.

In some families in Latin America there still unfortunately persists a chauvinist mentality that ignores the "newness" of Christianity, in which the equal dignity and responsibility of women relative to men is acknowledged and affirmed.

The family is irreplaceable for the personal serenity it provides and for the upbringing of children. Mothers who wish to dedicate themselves fully to bringing up their children and to the service of their family must enjoy conditions that make this possible, and for this they have the right to count on the support of the State. In effect, the role of the mother is fundamental for the future of society.

The father, for his part, has the duty to be a true father, fulfilling his indispensable responsibility and cooperating in bringing up the children. The children, for their integral growth, have a right to be able to count on their father and mother, who take care of them and accompany them on their way towards the fullness of life. Consequently there has to be intense and vigorous pastoral care of families. Moreover, it is indispensable to promote authentic family policies corresponding to the rights of the family as an essential subject in society. The family constitutes part of the good of peoples and of the whole of humanity.

Priests

The first promoters of discipleship and mission are those who have been called "to be with Jesus and to be sent out to preach" (cf. *Mk* 3:14), that is, *the priests*. They must receive preferential attention and paternal care from their Bishops, because they are the primary instigators of authentic renewal of Christian life among the People of God. I should like to offer them a word of paternal affection, hoping that "the Lord will be their portion and cup" (cf. *Ps* 16:5). If the priest has God as the foundation and centre of his life, he will experience the joy and the fruitfulness of his vocation. The priest must be above all a "man of

God" (*1 Tim* 6:11) who knows God directly, who has a profound personal friendship with Jesus, who shares with others the same sentiments that Christ has (cf. *Phil* 2:5). Only in this way will the priest be capable of leading men to God, incarnate in Jesus Christ, and of being the representative of his love. In order to accomplish his lofty task, the priest must have a solid spiritual formation, and the whole of his life must be imbued with faith, hope and charity. Like Jesus, he must be one who seeks, through prayer, the face and the will of God, and he must be attentive to his cultural and intellectual preparation.

Dear priests of this Continent, and those of you who have come here to work as missionaries, the Pope accompanies you in your pastoral work and wants you to be full of joy and hope; above all he prays for you.

Religious men and women and consecrated persons

I now want to address the religious men and women and consecrated members of the lay faithful. Latin American and Caribbean society needs your witness: in a world that so often gives priority to seeking well-being, wealth and pleasure as the goal of life, exalting freedom to the point where it takes the place of the truth of man created by God, you are witnesses that there is another meaningful way to live; remind your brothers and sisters that the Kingdom of God has already arrived; that justice and truth are possible if we open ourselves to the loving presence of God our Father, of Christ our brother and Lord, and of the Holy Spirit, our Comforter. With generosity and with heroism, you must continue working to ensure that society is ruled by love, justice, goodness, service and solidarity in conformity with the charism of your founders. With profound joy, embrace your consecration, which is an instrument of sanctification for you and of redemption for your brothers and sisters.

The Church in Latin America thanks you for the great work that you have accomplished over the centuries for the Gospel of Christ in favour of your brothers and sisters, especially the poorest and most deprived. I invite you always to work together with the Bishops and to work in unity with them, since they are the ones responsible for pastoral action. I exhort you also to sincere obedience towards the authority of the Church. Set yourselves no other goal than holiness, as you have learned from your founders.

The lay faithful

At this time when the Church of this Continent is committing herself whole-heartedly to her missionary vocation, I remind the lay faithful that they too are the

Church, the assembly called together by Christ so as to bring his witness to the whole world. All baptized men and women must become aware that they have been configured to Christ, the Priest, Prophet and Shepherd, by means of the common priesthood of the People of God. They must consider themselves jointly responsible for building society according to the criteria of the Gospel, with enthusiasm and boldness, in communion with their Pastors.

There are many of you here who belong to ecclesial movements, in which we can see signs of the varied presence and sanctifying action of the Holy Spirit in the Church and in today's society. You are called to bring to the world the testimony of Jesus Christ, and to be a leaven of God's love among others.

Young people and pastoral care of vocations

In Latin America the majority of the population is made up of young people. In this regard, we must remind them that their vocation is to be Christ's friends, his disciples. Young people are not afraid of sacrifice, but of a meaningless life. They are sensitive to Christ's call inviting them to follow him. They can respond to that call as priests, as consecrated men and women, or as fathers and mothers of families, totally dedicated to serving their brothers and sisters with all their time and capacity for dedication: with their whole lives. Young people must treat life as a continual discovery, never allowing themselves to be ensnared by current fashions or mentalities, but proceeding with a profound curiosity over the meaning of life and the mystery of God, the Creator and Father, and his Son, our Redeemer, within the human family. They must also commit themselves to a constant renewal of the world in the light of the Gospel. More still, they must oppose the facile illusions of instant happiness and the deceptive paradise offered by drugs, pleasure, and alcohol, and they must oppose every form of violence.

6. "Stay with us"

The deliberations of this Fifth General Conference lead us to make the plea of the disciples on the road to Emmaus our own: "Stay with us, for it is towards evening, and the day is now far spent" (*Lk* 24:29).

Stay with us, Lord, keep us company, even though we have not always recognized you. Stay with us, because all around us the shadows are deepening, and you are the Light; discouragement is eating its way into our hearts: make them burn with the certainty of Easter. We are tired of the journey, but you comfort us in the breaking of bread, so that we are able to proclaim to our brothers and sisters that you have truly risen and have entrusted us with the mission of being witnesses of your resurrection.

Stay with us, Lord, when mists of doubt, weariness or difficulty rise up around our Catholic faith; you are Truth itself, you are the one who reveals the Father to us: enlighten our minds with your word, and help us to experience the beauty of believing in you.

Remain in our families, enlighten them in their doubts, sustain them in their difficulties, console them in their sufferings and in their daily labours, when around them shadows build up which threaten their unity and their natural identity. You are Life itself: remain in our homes, so that they may continue to be nests where human life is generously born, where life is welcomed, loved and respected from conception to natural death.

Remain, Lord, with those in our societies who are most vulnerable; remain with the poor and the lowly, with indigenous peoples and Afro-Americans, who have not always found space and support to express the richness of their culture and the wisdom of their identity. Remain, Lord, with our children and with our young people, who are the hope and the treasure of our Continent, protect them from so many snares that attack their innocence and their legitimate hopes. O Good Shepherd, remain with our elderly and with our sick. Strengthen them all in faith, so that they may be your disciples and missionaries!

Conclusion

As I conclude my stay among you, I wish to invoke the protection of the Mother of God and Mother of the Church on you and on the whole of Latin America and the Caribbean. I beseech Our Lady in particular, under the title of Guadalupe, Patroness of America, and under the title of Aparecida, Patroness of Brazil, to accompany you in your exciting and demanding pastoral task. To her I entrust the People of God at this stage of the third Christian millennium. I also ask her to guide the deliberations and reflections of this General Conference and I ask her to bless with copious gifts the beloved peoples of this Continent.

Before I return to Rome I should like to leave a gift with the Fifth General Conference of the Bishops of Latin America and the Caribbean, to accompany and inspire them. It is this magnificent triptych from Cuzco, Peru, representing the Lord shortly before his Ascension into Heaven, as he is entrusting to his followers the mission to make disciples of all nations. The images evoke the close relationship linking Jesus Christ with his disciples and missionaries for the life of the world. The last panel represents Saint Juan

Diego proclaiming the Gospel, with the image of the Virgin Mary on his cloak and the Bible in his hand. The history of the Church teaches us that the truth of the Gospel, when our eyes take in its beauty and our minds and hearts receive it with faith, helps us to contemplate the dimensions of mystery that call forth our wonder and our adherence.

As I depart, I greet all of you most warmly and with firm hope in the Lord. Thank you very much!

It is love that gives life

There are no words to express my joy in being here with you to celebrate this solemn Eucharist on the occasion of the opening of the Fifth General Conference of the Bishops of Latin America and the Caribbean. I greet each of you most warmly ..... From this Shrine my thoughts reach out, full of affection and prayer, to all those who are spiritually united with us... To all I say: "Grace to you and peace from God our Father and the Lord Jesus Christ" (*1 Co*r 1:3).

I see it as a special gift of Providence that this Holy Mass is being celebrated *at this time and in this place*. The *time* is the liturgical season of Easter; on this Sixth Sunday of Easter, as Pentecost rapidly approaches, the Church is called to intensify her prayer for the coming of the Holy Spirit. The *place* is the National Shrine of Our Lady of Aparecida, the Marian heart of Brazil: Mary welcomes us to this *Upper Room* and, as our Mother and Teacher, helps us to pray trustingly to God with one voice. This liturgical celebration lays a most solid foundation for the Fifth Conference, setting it on the firm basis of prayer and the Eucharist, *Sacramentum Caritatis*. Only *the love of Christ*, poured out by the Holy Spirit, can make this meeting an authentic ecclesial event, a moment of grace for this Continent and for the whole world. This afternoon I will be able to discuss more fully the implications of the theme of your Conference. But now, let us leave space for the word of God which we have the joy of receiving with open and docile hearts, like Mary, Our Lady of the Immaculate Conception, so that, by the power of the Holy Spirit, Christ may once again take flesh in the "today" of our history.

The first reading, taken from the *Acts of the Apostles*, refers to the so-called "Council of Jerusalem", which dealt with the question as to whether the observance of the Mosaic Law was to be imposed on those pagans who had become Christians. The reading leaves out the discussion between "the apostles and the elders" (vv. 4-21) and reports the final decision, which was then written down in the form of a letter and entrusted to two delegates for delivery to the community in Antioch (vv. 22-29). This passage from Acts is highly appropriate for us, since we too are assembled here for an ecclesial meeting. It reminds us of the importance of community discernment with regard to the great problems and issues encountered by the Church along her way. These are clarified by the "apostles" and "elders" in the light of the Holy Spirit, who, as today's Gospel says, calls to mind the teaching of Jesus Christ (cf. *Jn* 14:26) and thus helps the Christian community to advance in charity towards the fullness of truth (cf. *Jn* 16:13). The Church's leaders discuss and argue, but in a constant attitude of religious openness to Christ's word in the Holy Spirit. Consequently, at the end they can say: "it has seemed good to the Holy Spirit and to us..." (*Acts* 15:28).

This is the "method" by which we operate in the Church, whether in small gatherings or in great ones. It is not only question of procedure: it is a reflection of the Church's very nature as a mystery of communion with Christ in the Holy Spirit. In the case of the General Conferences of the Bishops of Latin America and the Caribbean, the first, held in 1955 in Rio de Janeiro, merited a special Letter from Pope Pius XII, of venerable memory; in later Conferences, including the present one, the Bishop of Rome has travelled to the site of the continental gathering in order to preside over its initial phase. With gratitude and devotion let us remember the Servants of God Paul VI and John Paul II, who brought to the Conferences of Medellín, Puebla and Santo Domingo the witness of the closeness of the universal Church to the Churches in Latin America, which constitute, proportionally, the majority of the Catholic community.

"To the Holy Spirit and to us". This is the Church: we, the community of believers, the People of God, with its Pastors who are called to lead the way; together with the *Holy Spirit*, the Spirit of the Father, sent in the name of his Son Jesus, the Spirit of the one who is "greater" than all, given to us through Christ, who became "small" for our sake. The Paraclete Spirit, our *Ad-vocatus*, Defender and Consoler, makes us live in God's presence, as hearers of his word, freed from all anxiety and fear, bearing in our hearts the peace which Jesus left us, the peace that the world cannot give (cf. *Jn* 14:26-27). The Spirit accompanies the Church on her long pilgrimage between Christ's first and second coming. "I go away, and I will come to you" (*Jn* 14:28), Jesus tells his Apostles. Between Christ's "going away" and his "return" is the time of the Church, his Body. Two thousand years have passed so far, including these five centuries and more in which the Church has made her pilgrim way on the American Continent, filling believers with Christ's life through the sacraments and sowing in these lands the good seed of the Gospel, which has yielded thirty, sixty and a hundredfold. *The time of the Church, the time of the Spirit*: the Spirit is the Teacher who trains disciples: he teaches them to love Jesus; he trains them to hear his word and to contemplate his countenance; he

conforms them to Christ's sacred humanity, a humanity which is poor in spirit, afflicted, meek, hungry for justice, merciful, pure in heart, peacemaking, persecuted for justice's sake (cf. *Mt* 5:3-10). *By the working of the Holy Spirit, Jesus becomes the "Way" along which the disciple walks.* "If a man loves me, he will keep my word", Jesus says at the beginning of today's Gospel. "The word which you hear is not mine but the Father's who sent me" (*Jn* 14:23-24). Just as Jesus makes known the words of the Father, so the Spirit reminds the Church of Christ's own words (cf. *Jn* 14:26). And just as love of the Father led Jesus to feed on his will, so our love for Jesus is shown by our obedience to his words. Jesus' fidelity to the Father's will can be communicated to his disciples through the Holy Spirit, who pours the love of God into their hearts (cf. *Rom* 5:5).

The New Testament presents *Christ* as the *missionary of the Father.* Especially in the Gospel of John, Jesus often speaks of himself in relation to the Father who sent him into the world. And so in today's Gospel he says: "the word which you hear is not mine but the Father's who sent me" (*Jn* 14:24). At this moment, dear friends, we are invited to turn our gaze to him, for the Church's mission exists only as a prolongation of Christ's mission: "As the Father has sent me, even so I send you" (*Jn* 20:21). The evangelist stresses, in striking language, that the passing on of this commission takes place in the Holy Spirit: "he breathed on them and said to them: 'Receive the Holy Spirit'" (*Jn* 20:22). *Christ's mission is accomplished in love.* He has kindled in the world the fire of God's love (cf. *Lk* 12:49). *It is Love that gives life*: and so the Church has been sent forth to spread Christ's Love throughout the world, so that individuals and peoples "may have life, and have it abundantly" (*Jn* 10:10). To you, who represent the Church in Latin America, today I symbolically entrust my Encyclical *Deus Caritas Est*, in which I sought to point out to everyone the essence of the Christian message. The Church considers herself the *disciple and missionary of this Love*: missionary only insofar as she is a disciple, capable of being attracted constantly and with renewed wonder by the God who has loved us and who loves us first (cf. 1 *Jn* 4:10). The Church does not engage in proselytism. Instead, she grows by *"attraction"*: just as Christ "draws all to himself" by the power of his love, culminating in the sacrifice of the Cross, so the Church fulfils her mission to the extent that, in union with Christ, she accomplishes every one of her works in spiritual and practical imitation of the love of her Lord.

Dear brothers and sisters! This is the priceless treasure that is so abundant in Latin America, this is her most precious inheritance: *faith in the God who is Love*, who has shown us his face in Jesus Christ. You believe in the God who is Love: this is your strength, which overcomes the world, the joy that nothing and no one can ever take from you, the peace that Christ won for you by his Cross! *This is the faith that has made America the "Continent of Hope."* Not a political ideology, not a social movement, not an economic system: faith in the God who is Love – who took flesh, died and rose in Jesus Christ – is the authentic basis for this hope which has brought forth such a magnificent harvest from the time of the first evangelization until today, as attested by the ranks of Saints and *Beati* whom the Spirit has raised up throughout the Continent. Pope John Paul II called you to a *new evangelization*, and you accepted his commission with your customary generosity and commitment. I now confirm it with you, and in the words of this Fifth Conference I say to you: *be faithful disciples, so as to be courageous and effective missionaries.*

The second reading sets before us the magnificent vision of the *heavenly Jerusalem*. It is an image of awesome beauty, where nothing is superfluous, but everything contributes to the perfect harmony of the holy City. In his vision John sees the city "coming down out of heaven from God, having the glory of God" (*Rev* 21:10). And since the glory of God is Love, the heavenly Jerusalem is the icon of the Church, utterly holy and glorious, without spot or wrinkle (cf. *Eph* 5:27), permeated at her heart and in every part of her by the presence of the God who is Love. She is called a "bride", "the bride of the Lamb" (*Rev* 20:9), because in her is fulfilled the nuptial figure which pervades biblical revelation from beginning to end. The City and Bride is the locus of God's full communion with humanity; she has no need of a temple or of any external source of light, because the indwelling presence of God and of the Lamb illuminates her from within.

This magnificent icon has an *eschatological* value: it expresses the mystery of the beauty that is *already* the essential form of the Church, even if it has *not yet* arrived at its fullness. It is the goal of our pilgrimage, the homeland which awaits us and for which we long. Seeing that beauty with the eyes of faith, contemplating it and yearning for it, must not serve as an excuse for avoiding the historical reality in which the Church lives as she shares the joys and hopes, the grief and anguish of the people of our time, especially those who are poor or afflicted (cf. Constitution *Gaudium et Spes*, 1). If the beauty of the heavenly Jerusalem is the glory of God – his love in other words – then it is in charity, and in charity alone, that we can approach it and to a certain degree dwell within it even now. Whoever loves the Lord Jesus and keeps his word, already experiences in this world the mysterious presence of the Triune God. We heard this in the Gospel: "we will come to him and make our home with him" (*Jn* 14:23). Every Christian is therefore called to become a living stone of this splendid "dwelling place of God with men". What a magnificent vocation!

A Church totally enlivened and impelled by the love of Christ, the Lamb slain for love, is the image within history of the heavenly Jerusalem, prefiguring the holy city that is radiant with the glory of God. It releases *an irresistible missionary power* which is *the power of holiness*. Through the prayers of the Virgin Mary, may the Church in Latin America and the Caribbean be abundantly clothed with power from on high (cf. *Lk* 24:49), in order to spread throughout this Continent and the whole world the holiness of Christ. To him be glory, with the Father and the Holy Spirit, for ever and ever. Amen.

Sources

This booklet draws together homilies and addresses of Pope Benedict XVI during his Apostolic journey to Brazil on the occasion of the fifth General Conference of the Bishops of Latin America and the Caribbean in May 2007:

1. *Do you want life?* - Address of Benedict XVI to young people at the Municipal Stadium in Pacaembu, São Paulo, Thursday, 10 May 2007.

2. *Go out and bear fruit* - Homily of Benedict XVI during Holy Mass and Canonization of Fr Antonio de Sant'ana Galvão, OFM, "Campo de Marte", São Paulo, Friday, 11 May 2007.

3. *Proclaim the truth of our faith* - Address of Benedict XVI during the celebration of vespers with the Bishops of Brazil, Catedral da Sé, São Paulo, Friday, 11 May 2007.

4. *Hope does not disappoint* - Greeting of Benedict XVI to the Community of Poor Clares, Fazenda da Esperança, Guaratinguetá, Saturday, 12 May 2007.

5. *Be open to the desire for God* - Greeting of Benedict XVI to the community living in the Fazenda, Fazenda da Esperança, Guaratinguetá, Saturday, 12 May 2007.

6. *Being disciples of Christ today* - Address of Benedict XVI at the Inaugural Session of the fifth General Conference of the Bishops of Latin America and the Caribbean, Conference Hall, Shrine of Aparecida, Sunday, 13 May 2007.

7. *It is love that gives life* - Homily of Benedict XVI, Inauguration Mass of the fifth General Conference of the Bishops of Latin America and the Caribbean, Square in front of the Shrine of Aparecida, sixth Sunday of Easter, 13 May 2007.